ARM UP
SYSTEM

ARM UP SYSTEM

BY FRANK MITCHELL

Printed in the United States of America

First Printing, 2015

ISBN 978-0-692-59298-4

5280 Publishing, LLC
453 E. Wonderview Ave.
Estes Park, CO 80517
support@familysurvivalsystemsupport.com

DISCLAIMER OF LIABILITY AND WARRANTY

This publication describes the author's opinions regarding the subject matter herein. The author and publisher are not rendering advice or services pertaining to specific individuals or situations. For specific advice, or if expert assistance is required, the services of a qualified professional should be obtained.

The author and publisher assume no responsibility whatsoever for the use of the information in this publication or for decisions made or actions taken based, in whole or in part, on the information in this publication. The author and publisher make no warranties, express or implied, regarding the information. Without limiting the foregoing, the author and publisher specifically disclaim and will not be responsible for any liability, loss, or risk incurred directly, indirectly or incidentally as a consequence of the use or misuse of any advice or information presented herein. Use this publication and information with good judgment and do the best you can in your particular situation.

You agree to indemnify and hold the author and publisher, and their respective officers, directors, agents, employees, contractors and suppliers, harmless from any claim or demand, including reasonable attorneys' fees, related to your use or misuse of this publication or the information contained therein. You further agree that you will cooperate fully in the defense of any such claims. PLEASE CHECK YOUR LOCAL LAWS BEFORE USE OF THIS INFORMATION.

COPYRIGHT

TERMS AND DISCLAIMER

Table Of Contents

Why You Need This

The United States is facing an onslaught of draconian legislation meant to prevent law abiding citizens not only from purchasing new firearms, but also rendering illegal the firearms they already legally possess. We're of the opinion that these schemes will ultimately lead to nationwide registration, which can have only one end — confiscation. Regardless of what is uttered or written by the current administration, their sole goal is to take guns away from law abiding citizens.

Civilian disarmament has spanned many administrations, more or less starting with the National Firearms Act of 1934. Regulating firearms is not new, but consider that firearms laws work like a ratchet — *they only turn in one direction*, turning further and further away from the original intent of the Founding Fathers of this once great nation. Once in a while, the ratchet stops turning, and gun owners think that they have won a great victory — but it's not a victory, it's only a slowing of the creeping incrementalism that we have been subjected to. The recent *Heller* and *McDonald* Supreme Court decisions were lauded as a massive victory for the second amendment. We think that all these "landmark" decisions tell us what we already know — that the Second Amendment guarantees the individual right of keeping a firearm in the home for personal protection. And so the ratchet stopped turning for a while. It never turns back — it only stops, or turns forward.

What We Believe

We believe that if you are a law abiding citizen, with no criminal record that would otherwise prevent you from owning a firearm, that *you should be able to own whatever you like* and carry it *wherever you go*. We believe that if you are a felon or criminal, that you should never touch a firearm again, much less own one.

It's your 2nd Amendment right to own and use firearms and I intend to help you do that!

Why We're Writing This

We feel that the government of the United States as well as some individual state governments have conspired to strip you of your God given rights, so we're giving you some tools, some nuggets of wisdom so that you can beat them at their own game. We have put together an information packed manual on how you, the law abiding American citizen, can own firearms, avoid registration schemes, and take the fullest advantage of the firearms laws in this country. The better armed the citizenry is, the easier it will be to avoid federal tyranny. Use the knowledge herein to *legally* acquire as many firearms as you can before it's too late.

Understanding Firearms Laws

The chief agency that regulates firearms in the United States is the Bureau of Alcohol, Tobacco, Firearms, and Explosives, or BATFE. Often, this acronym is shortened to simply ATF, the designation the agency used to hold. Falling under the umbrella of the Department of Justice (DOJ), the ATF enforces firearms laws, among other things. The ATF is the chief enforcer of firearms commerce in America, and is responsible for licensing firearms dealers (referred to as Federal Firearms Licensees, or FFLs), auditing purchases of firearms, and ensuring that dealers and consumers comply with federal firearms laws.

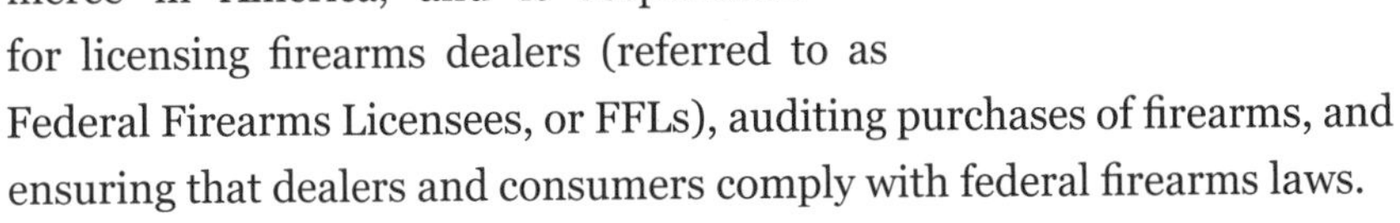

Unfortunately, the ATF also has a long and sordid history where it pertains to the enforcement of firearms laws; Randy Weaver, the main actor in the Ruby Ridge incident, was originally entrapped into selling two shotguns to a federal informant who was working for the ATF. The shotguns were minimally shorter than federal regulations permitted (though not of Weaver's doing), and after a series of events, the infa-

mous standoff ensued. Additionally, ATF was responsible for orchestrating the tragic loss of life that occurred at the Branch Davidian compound in Waco, Texas, when they attempted to execute a federal search warrant. Lately, ATF has also been behind the notorious Fast and Furious gun walking scandal, in which they allowed known straw purchasers to purchase guns illegally in the hopes of tracking these weapons. Instead of finding any meaningful leads to suspected cartel members, these illegally sold guns have been found at crime scenes on both sides of the US/Mexico border. While prosecuting the average American for minor infractions, the ATF, during Fast and Furious, let *thousands* of guns literally fall into the hands of cartel criminals. For an agency that is supposed to be dedicated to regulating firearms in America, the ATF is behind a surprising number of firearms debacles in which the agency itself breaks the laws it has been charged to enforce.

Still, to know and understand firearms laws, specifically, the laws enforced by the ATF, is to have power over the system currently in place. Agencies like the ATF count on gun owner apathy and general lack of knowledge of gun laws in order to further pressure owners into surrendering the guns they have, or scaring them into not buying new ones. Similarly, state governments and most law enforcement agencies are not particularly well versed in federal firearms laws, and make all sorts of mistakes in attempting to enforce the laws already on the books.

Again, to know the law is to have power over it. The first step in understanding firearms laws is to understand the nomenclature used. Consider that gun grabbers have come up with their own terminology in order to further confuse the masses. The media has appropriated these terms in an attempt to hijack lawful firearms ownership in the country and sway public opinion, as if public opinion has anything to do with the validity of the US Constitution. Here are a sampling of gun grabber terms and the translation:

Gun Grabber Term	Translation
Gun show loophole	The lawful transfer of firearms since the founding of the nation, between two parties, without ATF involvement
High capacity magazine	A standard capacity magazine
Assault Weapon	Your typical semiautomatic rifle, of which there are millions in the United states
Assault Clip	See high capacity magazine
Cop Killer Bullets	Standard hollow point ammunition
Common Sense	The opposite of what the Constitution says
High Powered	Standard powered, non magnum, small bore

It's important to never use terms like these, since they were invented by anti-gun activists and politicians whose only purpose is to divest you of your lawfully owned weapons and prevent you from buying more.

Curiously, though, most gun owners do not know the terms they *need to know* in order to properly understand the laws and thus use them to their advantage. The key term you need to acquaint yourself with is **Frame** or **Receiver**. While these terms are interchangeable, mostly people refer to frames on handguns and receivers on rifles or shotguns, but they are the same thing in practice. The ATF defines them as:

> **Frame or receiver:** That part of a firearm which provides housing for the hammer, bolt or breechblock and firing mechanism, and which is usually threaded at its forward portion to receive the barrel.

The reason why the receiver is so important is that it is the *actual firearm*, as defined by law. It is the controlled part that bears a serial number, and thus must be bought, sold, or transferred according to federal law. And herein lies the benefit to the knowledgeable gun owner.

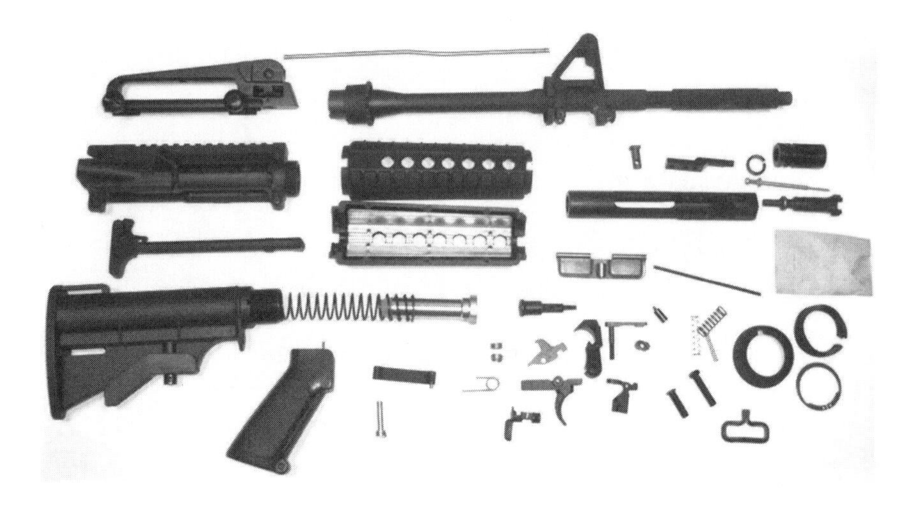

Take a close look at the picture above. Perhaps you are thinking that it's a disassembled AR 15 type rifle. Want to know what the ATF refers to it as? *Nothing*. It's just a bunch of parts, *none* of which are considered to be a firearm. Even if you were to assemble these parts, you still wouldn't have a firearm in the eyes of the ATF. Read on.

Now take a look at the picture below. What is it? If you said it's just a part, *you're wrong*. The "part" is in fact a lower receiver. *This part alone is the firearm*. In order to purchase this part from a Federal Firearms Dealer in all 50 states, you must fill out an ATF form 4473, pay a fee, and undergo a background check. In some states, you must even undergo a waiting period — all this for a piece of metal that can't shoot, can't accept ammunition, and isn't even a weapon at this stage — ah, but it's a *firearm*. Remember that. It will come into play later.

Here are some further images to clarify what we are speaking of:

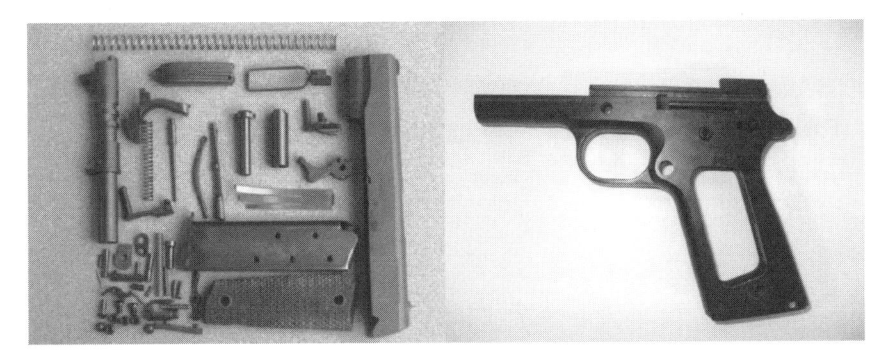

Not a firearm Firearm

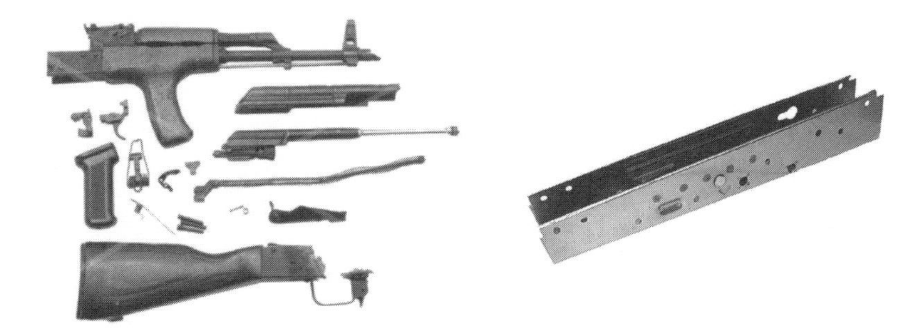

Not a firearm Firearm

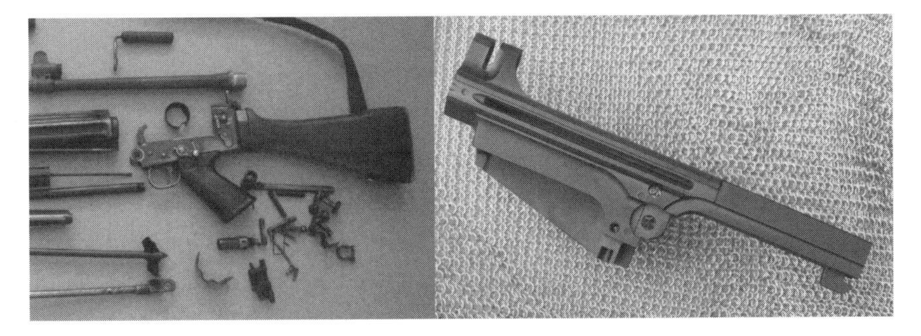

Not a firearm Firearm

We think you get the idea — a random collection of gun parts are just that — *gun parts*. Some gun parts, however, specifically, the receiver, are actual firearms and all federal and state laws apply to them.

So in theory, you could purchase a dozen AR-15 parts kits, minus the lower receivers, and not have to fill out a single form or tell anyone. And the ATF wouldn't care, either. Correct! *The ATF doesn't regulate gun parts, it regulates firearms.* So where do you get the receivers, in that case? Here are your options:

1. Buy them from a gun dealer, fill out a 4473, pay a fee, and undergo a background check.
2. Buy them from a private party (more about that later)
3. Build or make them

It's the third topic that we'll be speaking of in the next section....

Making Your Own Firearms

You can in fact make your own firearms from the ground up — as many as you want — and never have to deal with 4473s, dealers, paperwork, or even serial numbers. Anyone can actually make any firearm they want, providing that:

1. The person is not otherwise prohibited from owning a firearm
2. The firearm is not intended for sale (although it can be sold at a later date)
3. The person is not making a machine gun, short barreled shotgun, or any other NFA weapon (more about the NFA later)

As a matter of fact, the firearms you can make on your own *don't even need to have serial numbers* or markings of any kind. The applicable laws regarding making your own firearm are 18 U.S.C. 922(o) and (r), 26 U.S.C.5822, 27 CFR 478.39, 479.62 and 479.105. Search the United States Code for yourself at http://uscode.house.gov/

You can make your own gun 100% from scratch if you like, and if you possess the necessary expertise to do so. Plans of all kinds exist on the internet — many of them, however, are for machineguns and prohibited weapons, but hey — plans are plans. They are just drawings. Unless you actually build a prohibited firearm, it's impossible for you to run afoul of the law just by possessing schematics, jigs, or drawings.

Still, making your own functional firearm from plans is an onerous procedure, requiring quite a bit in the way of milling equipment, lathes, precision machinery, and most of all, know how. Sure, the British manufactured Sten Guns and other crude submachine guns during World War II, but we're guessing that some crude, inaccurate weapon is not really what you're after.

Wait — you don't need to make the whole gun — barrel, trigger, countless springs, pistol grip, etc — *you just have to make the receiver.* If you could make only the receiver of an AR, AK, or FAL type weapon, you could just buy all of the other non controlled parts! But doesn't it still take lots of work to make a receiver? Aren't there special tools and machining involved? Sure, if you were going to build a receiver from scratch — but there is something much better than that...

The 80% Receiver Or Frame

Recall that the receiver is the part of the firearm that is the serialized component and accepts the barrel as well as the fire control group. Still, that receiver, somewhere, starts out as a hunk of metal. A factory worker cuts a block of metal that is intended to be a receiver — is it still a firearm at that stage? Not until it is capable of receiving the fire control group and being functional as a firearm! So if you take that same cube of metal, and drill a single hole in it, is it a firearm? No! Okay, so how about if we take our raw cube of metal, and mill it down to the exact size of the receiver, and drill some holes in it — but not all the holes. Is it a firearm? No!

Take a close look at the above pictures — at first glance, they look like a lower receiver, but you know what the ATF calls them? *Hunks of metal.* Look closely, and you will see that the slot for the fire control group isn't milled out.

Additionally, none of the holes for the trigger or hammer pins have been drilled. This is what's called an *80% lower* because it's only 80% done. 80% receivers are to date available for all sorts of weapons — pistols such as 1911s, as well as rifles such as AK, AR, and FAL variants among others. There's a thriving market in 80% lowers today, because people want to take advantage of the many benefits an 80% receiver provides:

- Exempt from background checks, fees, or forms
- Can finish it off yourself
- Can be bought over the counter at will
- Totally anonymous and untraceable

Finishing off an 80% receiver to make it a 100% receiver is a task that varies in difficulty depending on what style receiver you are building; most 80% manufacturers also supply jigs and detailed plans for finishing the receiver off. Usually, the finish work on an 80% receiver can be done with some common hand tools and a drill press. Of course, one set of jigs can be used for *countless* 80% receivers, so they just about pay for themselves. When you're finished with an 80% receiver, you basically wind up with a 100% receiver, or a full on firearm. This part now becomes a controlled part just like any other store bought receiver. If you decide you want to sell it, you must properly mark the receiver with caliber and place of origin just like a store bought receiver has.

All said, a person could own a handful of 1911 pistols, an AK, a couple ARs, and an FAL without ever having made a purchase at a gun store save for parts, and without ever undergoing a background check or filling out a 4473. 80% receivers are a little bit of freedom that you can buy *today*, and finish with simple hand tools at home.

Additionally, if you are worried about registration schemes or people coming after the guns you already own, you could simply buy 80% receivers, finish them, and substitute them for the ones on your current guns. You could always surrender the receivers that came with your firearm, or destroy them.

A Word About Build Parties

In several states, overeager firearms owners have set up deals with machine shops in which a group of would-be receiver builders get together and mill a bunch of 80% lowers into firearms. Sometimes known as "build parties", some of these gatherings are so automated that the milling program for an 80% lower is even programmed into a CNC milling machine, so that all the person needs to do is clamp his 80% receiver into a jig, and push the button, causing the milling machine to do all the work. Sounds great, right? Push a button, get a firearm.

WRONG. This is a really slippery slope with questionable legality. Because the milling machine (or even machine shop for that matter) isn't owned by the person milling out the lower receiver, it can be postulated that the machine shop is now illegally manufacturing firearms. The ATF does not think that just because you pushed the button that initiated milling that you actually made the firearm yourself. This is such a massive gray area that we don't think its worth messing with. Avoid build parties, and mill out your own 80% lower receivers at home, by yourself, without assistance to comply with the spirit of the law and you'll be fine. It's not that hard!

3D Printers

The latest development on the 80% lower front, especially where it pertains to AR variants is the 3D printed lower. A 3D printer is a high tech printer that prints with liquid or melted plastic and is capable of making a three dimensional plastic piece of almost any shape. Naturally, gun enthusiasts have designed and successfully created AR lower receivers, of the 100% variety — printed firearms as it were. While 3D printers are mainly used for design prototyping, they are capable of being loaded with polymers of decent enough strength to make an AR lower. These printers are also not particularly expensive, with low end models selling for around $500.

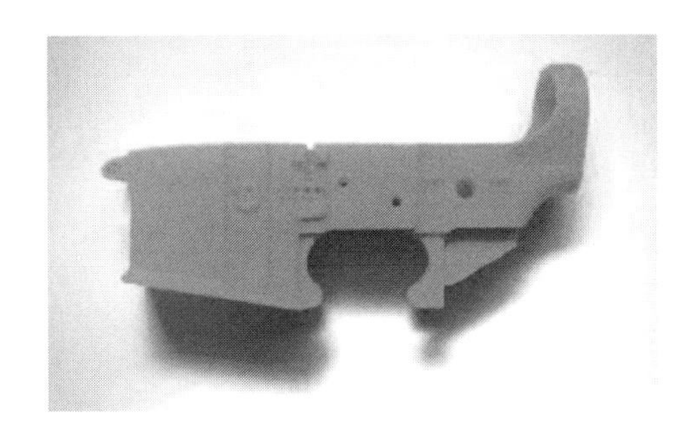

This is an extremely promising technology for AR enthusiasts; the AR's lower receiver houses the fire control group but doesn't really get subjected to the kind of stresses AR uppers take, and so it's a natural fit. One private individual claimed he shot 600 rounds through his printed receiver, and it was still going strong. It doesn't matter if it broke at 600 rounds — with a 3D printer, you could just print *more receivers*. The beauty of this is an unlimited supply of lowers, unregistered, of course.

The ATF has clarified their stance on 3D printed firearms in June of 2015. Turns out, there is a really old law on the books about "undetectable firearms". We won't bore you with the legalese, but the gist of the law states that no firearm may be manufactured that is undetectable to standard security detection systems (such as metal detectors, for example). Basically, since the 3D printed lower is made of plastic, it is essentially not detectable by a metal detector and therefore illegal.

Consider, however, that when assembled into a working firearm, the 3D printed lower will have lots of metal parts housed within it. The barrel and upper receiver will be metal. It is not "undetectable" at all. But remember, the ATF only considers the **lower** to be the firearm, and by itself, it is undetectable.

There is a workaround, however....permanently glue some pieces of metal to the 3D printed lower so that it is not undetectable. It's really pretty simple and satisfies that portion of the law. Think of the metal pieces as decorative trim, and go to town!

Buying Or Transferring A Gun Without A Background Check

For starters, purchasing a gun without a background check is already legal *in all 50 states* on a federal level. Dubbed the infamous "gun show loophole" this isn't a loophole at all – it has been in the gun control act since 1968 and essentially in practice since the foundation of the country. In the words of the ATF: *Any person may sell a firearm to an unlicensed resident of the State where he resides as long as he does not know or have reasonable cause to believe the person is prohibited from receiving or possessing firearms under Federal law.* 18 U.S.C. 922(a)(3) and (5), 922(d), 27 CFR 478.29 and 478.30

So if two consenting, law abiding adults meet at a gun show (or coffee shop, bullfighting ring, hardware store, discotheque, or anywhere else they feel like it), and one wants to sell the other a firearm, they can do the deal right there on the spot. Cash and carry. No papers, no registration, no background checks, nothing. This is federal law from time immemorial, not some random unknown loophole that crazy people are suddenly exploiting. The condition here is that *both parties must reside in the same state, and the transfer must occur within that state.* If one of the parties lives in a different state, or you want a gun that is for sale in a different state than where you are a resident, then you must still go through a licensed dealer to do the transfer, and you must undergo a background check.

Of course, some states have decided that they don't want honest, law abiding Americans transferring guns to each other, so they have preempted federal law by imposing their own laws. In California, for example, the right of private party transfers still exists, but both parties must execute the sale with the help of an FFL; the buyer must pay a fee, fill out a 4473, and undergo a background check.

The following states PROHIBIT private party transfers without a background check:

Hawaii	Illinois	Minnesota
California	Maryland	New Jersey
Colorado	Massachusetts	New York
Connecticut	Michigan	North Carolina

Keep a couple things in mind, however:

- Many states are considering or have passed bills that would prevent private parties from transferring firearms without bring the transaction through a licensed dealer and performing a background check.
- Some states have slight wrinkles in their laws — Oregon, for example, does not regulate private party firearms sales — except for when the purchase happens at a gun show.

When in doubt, check your local laws. So why would anyone want to buy a gun without a background check? Here's why:

- No meddling government to log the transaction.
- No registration of any kind
- No fees or forms to fill out
- Total anonymity in the transaction — you need not even exchange anything but first names.

Some people will say that it sounds "shady". The only reason it sounds that way is because the government has intentionally demonized gun owners as subversive and imminent law breakers, when in fact, every other product in America is bought this way. Lots of potential deadly weapons change hands without government interference every day — they're called cars. Why shouldn't guns be bought the same way?

Pre 1899 Firearms

What if there were guns you could buy, right now, that you could have mailed to your door, with no background check, no registration, or no paperwork? *What if these guns were not even considered to be firearms?* There is such a category, and they are referred to as *antique* guns by the ATF. They are quite literally firearms of all kinds that were manufactured before December 31, 1898, and there are a surprising number of them still in existence, and many still shoot very well.

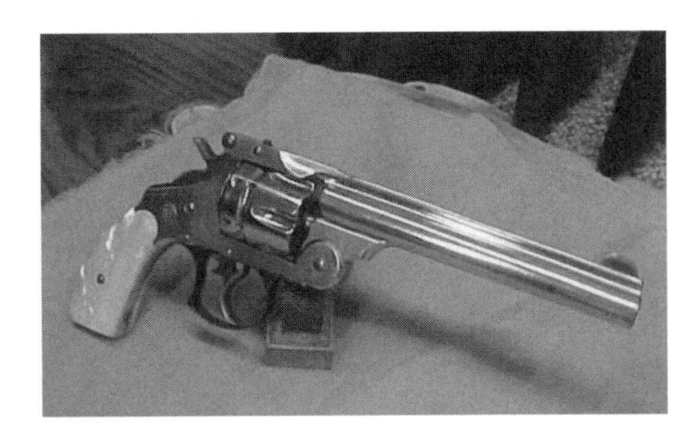

While some states still consider a pre 1899 firearm to still be a firearm (very few, in fact), most of them don't consider them to be a firearm at all. Additionally, these guns can be purchased in their original form, and then be re-chambered to a modern cartridge, and be just as functional as new guns. They can also be restocked or sporterized if you so wish.

There are some fantastic guns in this range, guns like Winchester Model 1897 12 gauge shotguns, Mauser bolt action rifles, Smith and Wesson double action revolvers, and of course Colt revolvers. They are still remarkably effective. Consider that pre 1899 firearms are:

- Not considered to be firearms
- Outside of federal jurisdiction
- Still available

- Free from registration or background check requirements
- In some states, can be carried concealed *as they are not considered to be firearms*...use your imagination.

I doubt anyone who was shot with a pre 1899 firearm would agree with the fact that it's "not considered to be a firearm"! Relevant code: 18 USC 921 (a)(16). Also consider that most firearms in general see very light use over their lifetimes. The main thing to look for in pre 1899 firearms isn't so much use as it is *wear*. Wear is caused by improper storage, corrosion, lack of lubrication, or finishes that have come off. Look for the guns that are in the best condition. There are entire businesses devoted to selling these, and they can guide you into the right purchase for you.

Black Powder Weapons

Sometimes overlapping with Antique weapons, but also with modern versions extant, there is a whole class of black powder weapons out there. Some of these black powder weapons are pistols, some are rifles — all of them use black powder. Before the emergence of modern smokeless powder, black powder ruled the battlefield. Black powder fueled the muskets of the revolutionary war as well as the muzzle loaders and rifled bore rifles of the civil war and beyond. Prior to self contained ammunition (i.e. cartridges) were common, cap and ball style weapons were the order of the day.

Once again, many black powder firearms aren't considered firearms by the federal government, and there are few to no restrictions on their purchase. Some states, however, have laws on the books regarding black powder firearms, but not that many of them. In fact, black powder pistols and muzzle loading rifles are often the choice of convicted felons who cannot otherwise own a firearm. While we don't necessarily agree with that position, there are some felons who were convicted of white collar crimes and things of that nature that we could see potentially wanting to own a firearm for self defense.

Let's face it — black powder weapons are not a perfect solution, but they can be *perfectly deadly* in the right hands. If you need proof of exactly how deadly black powder weapons can be, all you need to do is browse the pages of a history book and look up battles like Waterloo, Vicksburg, and Shiloh, where thousands upon thousands of men were killed by muzzle loading rifles, among other things. Loaded with a Minie Ball round and with a rifled barrel, a muzzle loader can be a remarkably deadly and accurate weapon, although slow to reload. Lastly, there are a whole slew of brand new black powder rifles and pistols available for sale for very little money. You don't even have to mess with antiques – you can get your black powder firearms brand new, and shipped to your door, with no background check or forms.

Gun Trusts

Most people are familiar with the legal mechanism of an ordinary trust; namely, it is an estate planning tool that is now being applied to gun purchases, and it works extremely well. A typical trust is made up of the *grantor*, who is the person who founds the trust and sets it up. Further, the grantor appoints a pool of *trustees*, who have the ability to use the assets of the trust. Lastly, the grantor appoints *beneficiaries*, who will assume the trust upon the passing of the grantor.

The interesting part is when, in accordance with federal law, the grantor purchases a firearm, and rather than registering the weapon in his own name, *he registers it in the name of the trust*. Let's look an example scenario:

Bill forms a gun trust, and appoints his wife, brother, best friend, and boss as a trustee. He also appoints his children and grandchildren as beneficiaries. He purchases ten guns. With this scenario:

- Any of the trustees may use the guns without having to be listed on the original registration.
- Upon Bill's passing, his children and then grandchildren will legally own the guns.
- None of the parties in the trust save Bill ever have to fill out a 4473 or any other registration document.

In the above scenario, Bill gets to control what happens to his guns, potentially beyond his own lifetime. Like the proverbial late night commercial – but wait, there's more! Gun trusts are excellent tools for the ownership of NFA weapons. National Firearms Act weapons, also known as Title 2 weapons are comprised of such things as:

- Machineguns
- Short barreled rifles
- Short barreled shotguns
- Sound suppressors and silencers

Most people are under the impression that these weapons are totally illegal for the average person to own, but most states allow NFA weapons if they are properly registered with the ATF, which requires:

- An application form
- A 2" x 2" color photograph
- Fingerprints
- A sign off from the local chief law enforcement officer of the locale in which you live (i.e. Chief of Police, County Sheriff)
- The payment of a $200 fee, per weapon.

Predictably, one of the biggest impediments to this process is the sign off by the chief law enforcement officer. Sheriff Bob just doesn't want you to have that belt fed .50 caliber machine gun you always dreamed of. Enter the gun trust: Because the weapon you are buying is registered to a trust, you no longer need fingerprints, a photograph, *or the sign off of the chief law enforcement officer!* You can tell him to go pound sand. Additionally, all members of the trust enjoy the use of the weapon as well, without them having to brave any lengthy application process or anything of that nature. Normally with NFA weapons, the only person that may have the weapon in their possession is the registered owner – severe penalties exist for someone having unlawful possession of an NFA weapon (try a $250,000 fine and a ten year, all expenses paid trip to Club Fed). With a gun trust, *anyone* can use or possess the weapons without the grantor being present.

The key to the effectiveness of trusts, besides the points mentioned above, is the fact that you don't need to deal with transfers between trustees and beneficiaries. With transfer laws at the center of impending legislation, it is conceivable that in the future, laws may be enacted which prevent transfers of firearms even *within families*. We know of one example where the California owner of a registered assault weapon passed away, and the weapon could not be transferred to his children because the statue of limitations to transfer that weapon had passed. It was surrendered to the police, and subsequently destroyed. A gun trust would have made the transfer totally seamless. Additionally, with magazines also being closely watched (specifically the standard capacity 30 round type), these too could be placed in the trust to be passed down to future generations, undoubtedly who will not have the freedom to buy their own. As most magazine laws contain grandfather clauses, this is an easy way to document the possession of magazines that might be illegal to buy or transfer in the future, and provide a way to get them to your loved ones easily.

Gun trusts form a subsection of estate law, and thus require a competent lawyer to set up. Thankfully, these are becoming more and more common, and the legal fees are reasonable ($500-$1500). Find an attorney that specializes in this area of law; your typical attorney knows little to nothing of firearms laws, much less machinegun laws. You want an expert to set this trust up — but the good news is that it can be multigenerational so that you are really paying once for something that can last a long, long time and derive you and your loved ones countless benefits.

Gun Trusts Under Attack

The concept of gun trusts is currently under attack, with the Obama regime actively looking to get the gun trust trustees to undergo background checks. It is possible in the future that the exemption that a gun trust has in not having to obtain the signature of the Chief Law Enforcement Officer of a jurisdiction to sign *may disappear*. The good news is that current gun trusts, both standard and NFA will remain active and will not have to undergo background checks. Get your gun trust up and running today, before it's too late!

In Closing

Use every *legal* means available to not only keep the guns you have, but purchase new ones. Your children might thank you some day! Always check your local laws for any variance from the federal law. Your local laws can normally be found on your State Attorney General's page.

If there is one takeaway from this guide it is to *avoid firearms registration at all costs*. Through the entirely legal mechanisms of private party transactions, 80% receivers, black powder weapons, pre 1899 firearms, and gun trusts, you are effectively removing the one single factor that will make confiscation easy — a permanent record of the firearms purchase transaction. Make no mistake; in the era of computerized records, any government agency that claims they delete records after a certain period of time is patently lying. There is no need to delete anything. And once they know you own a certain firearm, they will simply log it away. On the other hand, using the mechanisms that we've shown you, you can own virtually all the firearms you want with no government record thereof. That's liberty, and that's peace of mind.

Good luck!